IT'S TIME TO EAT BOK CHOY

It's Time to Eat
BOK CHOY

Walter the Educator

Silent King Books
A WhichHead Entertainment Imprint

Copyright © 2025 by Walter the Educator

All rights reserved. No part of this book may be reproduced in any manner whatsoever without written per- mission except in the case of brief quotations embodied in critical articles and reviews.

First Printing, 2024

Disclaimer

This book is a literary work; the story is not about specific persons, locations, situations, and/or circumstances unless mentioned in a historical context. Any resemblance to real persons, locations, situations, and/or circumstances is coincidental. This book is for entertainment and informational purposes only. The author and publisher offer this information without warranties expressed or implied. No matter the grounds, neither the author nor the publisher will be accountable for any losses, injuries, or other damages caused by the reader's use of this book. The use of this book acknowledges an understanding and acceptance of this disclaimer.

It's Time to Eat BOK CHOY is a collectible early learning book by Walter the Educator suitable for all ages belonging to Walter the Educator's Time to Eat Book Series. Collect more books at WaltertheEducator.com

USE THE EXTRA SPACE TO TAKE NOTES AND DOCUMENT YOUR MEMORIES

BOK CHOY

It's time to eat, hooray, hooray!
\

It's Time to Eat

Bok Choy

A crunchy treat is on the way!

Green on top and white below,

Bok choy is the way to go!

Tall and leafy, crisp and bright,

Pick it fresh, oh, what a sight!

Wash it clean, then chop, chop, chop,

Into the pan, plop, plop, plop!

Sizzle, sizzle in the pot,

Steam it, stir it, serve it hot!

Add some sauce or eat it plain,

Bok choy's flavor is never plain!

Try it raw with dips so sweet,

A tasty snack that's hard to beat!

Crunchy, munchy, fresh and cool,

Bok choy makes a perfect fuel!

It's Time to Eat

Bok Choy

Put it in a soup so warm,

Or in noodles, soft or firm!

Toss it in a stir-fry too,

Bok choy's great in all you do!

Did you know it's good for you?

Helps you grow up strong and true!

Full of goodness, full of cheer,

Eat bok choy all through the year!

Leaves so tender, stalks so white,

Bok choy brings such pure delight!

Mild and mellow, soft yet crisp,

Every bite is just like this!

Some like big ones, some like small,

Some eat lots, some eat them all!

Any way you like to chew,

It's Time to Eat

Bok Choy

Bok choy's fun for me and you!

Try a bite and you will see,

Bok choy's tasty as can be!

Crunch and munch, then have some more,

A veggie snack you will adore!

So grab a plate and take a try,

Bok choy's great, don't be shy!

Eat it up and shout, "Hooray!"

It's Time to Eat

Bok Choy

Bok choy time is here today!

ABOUT THE CREATOR

Walter the Educator is one of the pseudonyms for Walter Anderson. Formally educated in Chemistry, Business, and Education, he is an educator, an author, a diverse entrepreneur, and he is the son of a disabled war veteran. "Walter the Educator" shares his time between educating and creating. He holds interests and owns several creative projects that entertain, enlighten, enhance, and educate, hoping to inspire and motivate you. Follow, find new works, and stay up to date with Walter the Educator™

at WaltertheEducator.com

www.ingramcontent.com/pod-product-compliance
Lightning Source LLC
LaVergne TN
LVHW052011060526
838201LV00059B/3962